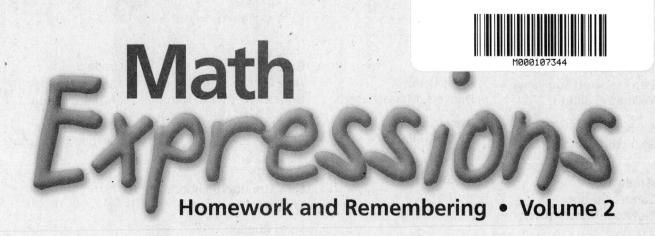

Math Expressions

Homework and Remembering • Volume 2

Developed by
The Children's Math Worlds Research Project

PROJECT DIRECTOR AND AUTHOR
Dr. Karen C. Fuson

This material is based upon work supported by the
National Science Foundation
under Grant Numbers
ESI-9816320, REC-9806020, and RED-935373.

Any opinions, findings, and conclusions, or recommendations expressed in this material
are those of the author and do not necessarily reflect the views of the National Science Foundation.

HOUGHTON MIFFLIN HARCOURT

Teacher Reviewers

Kindergarten
Patricia Stroh Sugiyama
Wilmette, Illinois

Barbara Wahle
Evanston, Illinois

Grade 1
Sandra Budson
Newton, Massachusetts

Janet Pecci
Chicago, Illinois

Megan Rees
Chicago, Illinois

Grade 2
Molly Dunn
Danvers, Massachusetts

Agnes Lesnick
Hillside, Illinois

Rita Soto
Chicago, Illinois

Grade 3
Jane Curran
Honesdale, Pennsylvania

Sandra Tucker
Chicago, Illinois

Grade 4
Sara Stoneberg Llibre
Chicago, Illinois

Sheri Roedel
Chicago, Illinois

Grade 5
Todd Atler
Chicago, Illinois

Leah Barry
Norfolk, Massachusetts

Credits

Cover art: (t) © Charles Cormany/Workbook Stock/Jupiter Images

Ilustrative art: Robin Boyer/Deborah Wolfe, LTD; Geoff Smith, Tim Johnson
Technical art: Nesbitt Graphics, Inc.
Photos: Nesbitt Graphics, Inc.

ISBN: 978-0-547-47918-7

9 10 11 12 13 0304 21 20 19 18 17

4500679439   X B C D E

Name _____

Homework

Draw one diagonal.	Draw the other diagonal.	Draw both diagonals.
I.		
2.		
3.		
4.		

5. **On the Back** Find an object in your home that is a quadrilateral and use a ruler to draw a picture of it. Draw two diagonals. What shapes did you form by drawing the two diagonals?

Diagonals of Quadrilaterals

Homework

Use estimation to find the midpoints.

Connect the midpoints of two opposite sides.	Connect the midpoints of the other two sides.	Draw both line segments.
1.		
2.		
3.		

➡ **4. On the Back** Find an object in the shape of a quadrilateral in your home.

- Use a centimeter ruler to draw the object.
- Estimate the position of the midpoint on each side.
- Connect the midpoints of opposite sides.
- Describe the shapes that you see.

Homework

Draw one diagonal.	Draw the other diagonal.	Draw both diagonals.
I.		
2.		

Use estimation to find the midpoints.

Connect the midpoints of two opposite sides.	Connect the midpoints of the other two sides.	Draw both line segments.
3.		
4.		

5. On the Back For each shape above, tell about the new shapes you made.

Practice with Diagonals and Connecting Midpoints

Name _____

Homework

Draw coins to show 6 different ways to make 25¢
with pennies, nickels, and/or dimes.

1. 25¢	2. 25¢	3. 25¢
4. 25¢	5. 25¢	6. 25¢

Write how to count the money.

7.

  <u>25¢</u>   <u>50¢</u>   ___   ___   ___   ___   ___   ___   ___

8.

  <u>25¢</u>   <u>50¢</u>   ___   ___   ___   ___   ___

Targeted Practice

Use the bar graph to answer the questions below. Write your answers in the boxes. Ring *more* or *fewer*.

Number of Pets in the Pet Store

1. There are [ ] *more fewer* birds in the pet store than lizards.

2. There are [ ] *more fewer* puppies in the pet store than kittens.

3. There are [ ] *more fewer* fish in the pet store than birds.

4. There are [ ] *more fewer* lizards in the pet store than kittens.

5. There are [ ] *more fewer* puppies in the pet store than fish.

6. There are *more fewer* fish than there are birds and lizards combined.

7. There is a total of [ ] puppies and kittens.

Explore Quarters

Homework

Draw coins to show 6 different ways to make $1.00.
Use pennies, nickels, dimes, and/or quarters.

1. $1.00	2. $1.00
3. $1.00	4. $1.00
5. $1.00	6. $1.00

Name _____

Remembering

Complete the number sequence. Write the rule.

1. 75, 69, 63, _____, _____, _____   Rule: n _____

2. 34, 41, 48, _____, _____, _____   Rule: n _____

Add.

3. $100 + 71 =$ _____ $6 + 100 =$ _____

   $10 + 71 =$ _____ $6 + 10 =$ _____

   $1 + 71 =$ _____ $6 + 1 =$ _____

Add.

4. $\begin{array}{r} 73 \\ + 30 \\ \hline \end{array}$ 5. $\begin{array}{r} 64 \\ + 99 \\ \hline \end{array}$ 6. $\begin{array}{r} 26 \\ + 58 \\ \hline \end{array}$

Solve the story problem.   **Show your work.**

7. Mr. Green worked at the store 57
   hours last week. Mrs. Green
   worked the same number of hours.
   How many hours did they work in
   total?

    _____
                          label

8. **Geometry** Draw a diagonal.

Explore Dollars

Name _____

Homework

Solve the story problems. Rewrite the 100 or make
a drawing. Add to check your answer.

$$100 = \overset{90}{\cancel{100}} + \overset{10}{\cancel{0}}$$
$$-\ 68 = \quad 60 + 8$$
$$\overline{\qquad\qquad 30 + 2 = 32}$$

Tens	Ones
9	10

$$\overset{9\ 10}{\cancel{100}}$$
$$-\ \ 68$$
$$\overline{\quad 32}$$

---

1. There were 100 rubber ducks in the
river race. 19 of them sank. How
many ducks are in the race now?

☐   _____
           label

---

2. Ben bought 100 napkins for the
picnic. We used 74 of them. How
many napkins were left?

☐   _____
           label

Find the unknown partner. Check by adding.

3.

Targeted Practice

Use the information in the circle graph to answer the questions below. Fill in the blanks.

**Weather This Month
(Number of Days)**

1. We had _____ on more days than any other kind of weather.

2. We had rain 1 more day than we had _____.

3. We had snow 4 fewer days than we had _____.

4. We had wind 5 more days than we had _____.

5. We had sun and snow for the same total number of days as we had _____ and _____.

Write two other things the circle graph shows.

_____

_____

_____

_____

_____

_____

Homework

Solve each story problem. Make a
proof drawing if you need to.

Show your work.

1. Amon had 94 tomato seeds. He
   used 27 of them for a science
   project. How many seeds did he
   have left?

   ☐ _____
   label

2. Benita made 56 leaf prints. She
   gave 29 prints to her cousins. How
   many prints does Benita have now?

   ☐ _____
   label

3. Denise had 71 straws. She used 33
   of them to make a bridge. How
   many straws does she have left?

   ☐ _____
   label

4. Cedric had 70 sports cards. He
   gave away 24 cards to his friends.
   How many cards does Cedric have
   now?

   ☐ _____
   label

Remembering

Add.

1. 45
    + 93

2. 72
    + 59

3. 48
    + 23

4. Draw coins to show two ways to make 25¢.

┌─────────────────────┐   ┌─────────────────────┐
│   25¢   │   │   25¢   │
│   │   │   │
│   │   │   │
│   │   │   │
│   │   │   │
└─────────────────────┘   └─────────────────────┘

Solve the story problem.   **Show your work.**

5. Josh solved 8 math problems. If he
   had solved another 7 problems he
   would have solved as many as
   Mato. How many problems did
   Mato solve?

   ┌──────┐ _____
   │   │
   └──────┘   label

6. Geometry

Connect midpoints of two opposite sides.	Connect midpoints of the other two opposite sides.	Draw both line segments.

Name

Homework

The Expanded Method	The Ungrouping First Method	Proof Drawing

$$93 = 90 + 3 \quad (80 + 13)$$
$$-57 = 50 + 7$$
$$\overline{} \quad 30 + 6 = 36$$

$$
\begin{array}{r} 93 \\ -57 \\ \hline 36 \end{array}
$$

Subtract using any method.

1. $\begin{array}{r} 3\,8 \\ -2\,1 \\ \hline \end{array}$

2. $\begin{array}{r} 5\,7 \\ -3\,9 \\ \hline \end{array}$

3. $\begin{array}{r} 9\,5 \\ -6\,4 \\ \hline \end{array}$

4. $\begin{array}{r} 5\,0 \\ -1\,3 \\ \hline \end{array}$

5. $\begin{array}{r} 6\,8 \\ -1\,5 \\ \hline \end{array}$

6. $\begin{array}{r} 7\,7 \\ -2\,9 \\ \hline \end{array}$

7. $\begin{array}{r} 7\,4 \\ -4\,8 \\ \hline \end{array}$

8. $\begin{array}{r} 8\,4 \\ -4\,9 \\ \hline \end{array}$

Targeted Practice

Subtract.

1. 64
   − 37
   _____

2. 81
   − 34
   _____

3. 48
   − 26
   _____

4. 73
   − 19
   _____

5. 96
   − 58
   _____

6. 55
   − 26
   _____

7. 67
   − 52
   _____

8. 71
   − 45
   _____

9. 43
   − 15
   _____

10. 38
    − 14
    _____

11. 50
    − 31
    _____

12. 94
    − 57
    _____

13. 76
    − 38
    _____

14. 85
    − 67
    _____

15. 84
    − 49
    _____

Two Methods of Subtraction

Homework

Subtract.

1. $\begin{array}{r} 87 \\ -59 \\ \hline \end{array}$

2. $\begin{array}{r} 63 \\ -14 \\ \hline \end{array}$

3. $\begin{array}{r} 55 \\ -18 \\ \hline \end{array}$

4. $\begin{array}{r} 73 \\ -17 \\ \hline \end{array}$

5. $\begin{array}{r} 83 \\ -12 \\ \hline \end{array}$

6. $\begin{array}{r} 99 \\ -35 \\ \hline \end{array}$

7. $\begin{array}{r} 62 \\ -55 \\ \hline \end{array}$

8. $\begin{array}{r} 71 \\ -49 \\ \hline \end{array}$

9. $\begin{array}{r} 45 \\ -26 \\ \hline \end{array}$

10. $\begin{array}{r} 50 \\ -11 \\ \hline \end{array}$

11. $\begin{array}{r} 92 \\ -44 \\ \hline \end{array}$

12. $\begin{array}{r} 75 \\ -52 \\ \hline \end{array}$

Remembering

Answer the questions below by reading the circle graph.

1. How many chickens and ducks are there altogether on the farm?

Animals on the Farm

_____
label

2. How many more cows are there than sheep?

_____
label

3. How many fewer pigs are there than chickens?

_____
label

Subtract.

4. 9 1
  − 5 2

5. 8 7
  − 3 6

6. 7 0
  − 2 3

7. Geometry

Draw one diagonal.	Draw the other diagonal.	Draw both diagonals.

Practice and Explain a Method

Name _____

Homework

Solve each story problem. Draw a
proof drawing if you need to.

Show your work.

1. There were 200 water bottles on a
   table. The runners in a race took 73
   of them. How many water bottles
   are left on the table?

   ┌─────────┐
   │   │ _____
   └─────────┘
       label

2. There were 200 weeds in my
   garden. My little sister pulled out 68
   of them. How many weeds are still
   in the garden?

   ┌─────────┐
   │   │ _____
   └─────────┘
       label

Subtract.

3. $\begin{array}{r} 200 \\ -\ 66 \\ \hline \end{array}$

4. $\begin{array}{r} 200 \\ -\ 82 \\ \hline \end{array}$

5. $\begin{array}{r} 200 \\ -\ 68 \\ \hline \end{array}$

6. $\begin{array}{r} 200 \\ -\ 95 \\ \hline \end{array}$

7. $\begin{array}{r} 200 \\ -\ 72 \\ \hline \end{array}$

8. $\begin{array}{r} 200 \\ -\ 47 \\ \hline \end{array}$

Name _____

Targeted Practice

Subtract.

1. $\begin{array}{r} 164 \\ -\ 53 \\ \hline \end{array}$

2. $\begin{array}{r} 136 \\ -\ 73 \\ \hline \end{array}$

3. $\begin{array}{r} 157 \\ -\ 65 \\ \hline \end{array}$

4. $\begin{array}{r} 145 \\ -\ 83 \\ \hline \end{array}$

5. $\begin{array}{r} 187 \\ -\ 44 \\ \hline \end{array}$

6. $\begin{array}{r} 138 \\ -\ 56 \\ \hline \end{array}$

7. $\begin{array}{r} 168 \\ -\ 42 \\ \hline \end{array}$

8. $\begin{array}{r} 123 \\ -\ 61 \\ \hline \end{array}$

9. $\begin{array}{r} 114 \\ -\ 72 \\ \hline \end{array}$

10. $\begin{array}{r} 187 \\ -\ 93 \\ \hline \end{array}$

11. $\begin{array}{r} 199 \\ -\ 88 \\ \hline \end{array}$

12. $\begin{array}{r} 175 \\ -\ 94 \\ \hline \end{array}$

Subtract from 200

Homework

Decide if you need to ungroup. Then subtract.

1. $\begin{array}{r} 147 \\ -\ 32 \\ \hline \end{array}$

2. $\begin{array}{r} 147 \\ -\ 38 \\ \hline \end{array}$

3. $\begin{array}{r} 147 \\ -\ 48 \\ \hline \end{array}$

4. $\begin{array}{r} 126 \\ -\ 54 \\ \hline \end{array}$

5. $\begin{array}{r} 126 \\ -\ 57 \\ \hline \end{array}$

6. $\begin{array}{r} 126 \\ -\ 97 \\ \hline \end{array}$

7. $\begin{array}{r} 187 \\ -\ 46 \\ \hline \end{array}$

8. $\begin{array}{r} 187 \\ -\ 49 \\ \hline \end{array}$

9. $\begin{array}{r} 187 \\ -\ 99 \\ \hline \end{array}$

10. $\begin{array}{r} 172 \\ -\ 35 \\ \hline \end{array}$

11. $\begin{array}{r} 172 \\ -\ 85 \\ \hline \end{array}$

12. $\begin{array}{r} 172 \\ -\ 31 \\ \hline \end{array}$

Name _____

Remembering

Solve the story problem.   **Show your work.**

1. The baker made 67 muffins in the
   morning. He plans to make 93
   more. How many muffins will he
   make if he follows his plan?

   ┌──────────┐
   │   │ _____
   └──────────┘
              label

Use the picture graph to answer the questions.

Bikes in the Garage

Mike	🚲	🚲	🚲	🚲						
Christy	🚲	🚲	🚲	🚲	🚲	🚲	🚲	🚲		
Sarah	🚲	🚲								

2. How many more bikes does Christy have than Sarah? _____ bikes

3. How many fewer bikes does Sarah have than Mike? _____ bikes

4. **Geometry**

Connect midpoints of two opposite sides.	Connect midpoints of the other two opposite sides.	Draw both line segments.
☐	☐	☐

Name _____

Homework

Decide if you need to ungroup. Then subtract.

1. $\begin{array}{r} 1\,3\,0 \\ -\ \ 9\,9 \\ \hline \end{array}$

2. $\begin{array}{r} 1\,5\,0 \\ -\ \ 3\,9 \\ \hline \end{array}$

3. $\begin{array}{r} 1\,6\,0 \\ -\ \ 6\,7 \\ \hline \end{array}$

4. $\begin{array}{r} 1\,0\,8 \\ -\ \ 8\,8 \\ \hline \end{array}$

5. $\begin{array}{r} 1\,2\,0 \\ -\ \ 8\,3 \\ \hline \end{array}$

6. $\begin{array}{r} 1\,0\,1 \\ -\ \ 7\,2 \\ \hline \end{array}$

Solve each story problem. **Show your work.**

7. There were 120 nickels in a jar. Janice took out 49. How many nickels are in the jar now?

label

8. 109 books were sent to the bookstore last Saturday. So far, 25 have been sold. How many have not been sold?

label

Name _____

Targeted Practice

Subtract.

1.   116
  − 37
  _____

2.   148
  − 65
  _____

3.   176
  − 89
  _____

4.   163
  − 18
  _____

5.   123
  − 65
  _____

6.   104
  − 12
  _____

7.   124
  − 39
  _____

8.   170
  − 97
  _____

9.   133
  − 35
  _____

10.   117
  − 54
  _____

11.   124
  − 35
  _____

12.   146
  − 17
  _____

Zero in the Ones or Tens Place

Homework

What would you like to buy? First, see how much
money you have. Pay for the item. How much money
will you have left?

Yard Sale

Globe	Ring	Sports Bag	Eraser	Colored Pencils
85¢	67¢	98¢	79¢	66¢

---

1. I have 124¢ in my pocket.
I bought the _____.

```
  1 2 4¢
-     ¢
_____
```

I have _____ ¢ left.

2. I have 152¢ in my pocket.
I bought the _____.

```
  1 5 2¢
-     ¢
_____
```

I have _____ ¢ left.

---

3. I have 145¢ in my pocket.
I bought the _____.

```
  1 4 5¢
-     ¢
_____
```

I have _____ ¢ left.

4. I have 131¢ in my pocket.
I bought the _____.

```
  1 3 1¢
-     ¢
_____
```

I have _____ ¢ left.

Name

Remembering

Subtract.

1. 103
   − 55

2. 150
   − 91

3. 170
   − 93

4. 140
   − 54

5. 109
   − 22

6. 108
   − 49

Write the time on the digital clock.

7.

8.

9.

10.

11. Geometry

Draw one diagonal.	Draw the other diagonal.	Draw both diagonals.

Model Subtraction with Money

Homework

Draw a Math Mountain to solve each story problem. Show how you add or subtract.

Show your work.

1. Papi had 148 slices of pizza in his shop. He sold 56 slices. How many slices does Papi have left?

   [ ] _____

   label

2. There were 84 children at the park. Then 61 children joined them. How many children are at the park now?

   [ ] _____

   label

3. Bella had 119 crayons. She gave 36 of them to her friend. How many crayons did she have left?

   [ ] _____

   label

4. Luke ran for 79 minutes. Then he swam for 48 minutes. How many minutes did Luke spend doing these two things?

   [ ] _____

   label

Targeted Practice

Solve each story problem.   **Show your work.**

1. Lena solved a math puzzle in 87 seconds. She solved another puzzle in 63 seconds. How many seconds did it take her to solve both puzzles?

   [ ] _____
              label

2. Lori built a tower with 147 blocks. 59 of the blocks fell off. How many blocks are in the tower now?

   [ ] _____
              label

3. The library owns 113 art books. 74 of them are checked out. How many art books are still in the library?

   [ ] _____
              label

4. My dog Max has 26 spots on him. My other dog, Lucky, has 58 spots on him. How many spots do my dogs have on them?

   [ ] _____
              label

Story Problems with Addition and Subtraction

Name _____

Homework

1. Write all of the equations for 74, 25, and 49.

$25 + 49 = 74$ $74 = 25 + 49$

_____   _____

_____   _____

_____   _____

2. Write all the equations for 157, 68, and 89.

$68 + 89 = 157$ $157 = 68 + 89$

_____   _____

_____   _____

_____   _____

Name _____

Remembering

Add or subtract.

1.
```
  2 0 0
-   6 9
```
```
  1 7 3
-   4 8
```
```
   3 8
+  4 9
```

Use the information in the bar graph to answer
these questions.

Bugs I Saw in My Yard

2. How many more butterflies did I see
   than bees?

   ┌──────────┐
   │   │ _____
   └──────────┘   label

3. How many fewer ants did I see than
   beetles?

   ┌──────────┐
   │   │ _____
   └──────────┘   label

4. How many beetles and wasps did I see in my yard?

   ┌──────────┐
   │   │ _____
   └──────────┘   label

5. Draw both diagonals.

   ┌──────────────────┐
   │   │
   │   │
   │   │
   └──────────────────┘

Math Mountain Equations with Larger Numbers

Homework

Add or subtract. Watch the sign!

1.
$$\begin{array}{r} 75 \\ +28 \\ \hline \end{array}$$

2.
$$\begin{array}{r} 133 \\ -85 \\ \hline \end{array}$$

3.
$$\begin{array}{r} 47 \\ +98 \\ \hline \end{array}$$

4.
$$\begin{array}{r} 87 \\ -48 \\ \hline \end{array}$$

5.
$$\begin{array}{r} 34 \\ +18 \\ \hline \end{array}$$

6.
$$\begin{array}{r} 162 \\ -84 \\ \hline \end{array}$$

7.
$$\begin{array}{r} 76 \\ +93 \\ \hline \end{array}$$

8.
$$\begin{array}{r} 156 \\ -29 \\ \hline \end{array}$$

9.
$$\begin{array}{r} 58 \\ +95 \\ \hline \end{array}$$

10.
$$\begin{array}{r} 121 \\ -53 \\ \hline \end{array}$$

11.
$$\begin{array}{r} 96 \\ +37 \\ \hline \end{array}$$

12.
$$\begin{array}{r} 101 \\ -39 \\ \hline \end{array}$$

Name _____

Targeted Practice

Solve each story problem.   **Show your work.**

1. The doll shop had 72 new dolls.
   They sold 34 of them. How many
   dolls does the shop have left?

   [___] _____
              label

2. I collected 95 stickers. My sister
   collected 48 stickers. How many
   stickers did my sister and I collect
   in all?

   [___] _____
              label

3. At the dance studio, 67 girls and 86
   boys signed up for lessons. In total,
   how many children signed up for
   dance lessons?

   [___] _____
              label

4. For the picnic, we bought 153 cups.
   Only 78 of them were used. How
   many cups are left over?

   [___] _____
              label

Practice Addition and Subtraction

Name _____

Homework

Mr. Green wants to buy some things at a flea market.
He will pay for the items with two dollars (200 cents).
How much change will he get back?

| Mittens 57¢ | Toy Binoculars 89¢ | Toy Camera 96¢ | Toy Lamb 78¢ | Plant 65¢ |

1. Mr. Green buys the mittens and the plant.

_____ ¢

+ _____ ¢

Total: _____

200¢ − _____ = _____

His change will be _____ ¢.

2. Mr. Green buys the toy lamb and the toy camera.

_____ ¢

+ _____ ¢

Total: _____

200¢ − _____ = _____

His change will be _____ ¢.

3. Mr. Green buys the toy binoculars and the toy lamb.

_____ ¢

+ _____ ¢

Total: _____

200¢ − _____ = _____

His change will be _____ ¢.

4. Mr. Green buys the toy camera and the plant.

_____ ¢

+ _____ ¢

Total: _____

200¢ − _____ = _____

His change will be _____ ¢.

Name _____

Remembering

1. Write all of the equations for 142, 58, and 84.

$$142 = 58 + 84$$ _____ $$58 + 84 = 142$$ _____

_____   _____

_____   _____

2. What time is it? Write the time on the digital clock.

Solve the story problem.   **Show your work.**

3. In the morning Kevin counted 121 trucks and 53 cars. In the afternoon he counted 68 trucks and 95 cars. How many trucks did he count altogether?

[   ] _____
          label

Buy and Sell with Two Dollars

Name _____

Homework

Add on to solve each story problem.

Show your work.

1. Rudy had 72 ants in his ant farm. He added some more ants. Now there are 209 ants. How many ants did Rudy add?

   [ ]   _____

   label

2. Tina had 92 flowers in her garden this morning. After she took some to school, she had 33 flowers. How many flowers did Tina take to school?

   [ ]   _____

   label

3. Lia collected 119 pins. Then she gave some to Matt. Now Lia has 58 pins. How many pins did Lia give to Matt?

   [ ]   _____

   label

4. There were 124 cars in the garage this morning. Now there are 66 cars in the garage. How many cars left the garage?

   [ ]   _____

   label

Name _____

Targeted Practice

The train stops at the streets shown in the table. Tell the ticket collector where you would like to go. Pay for your ticket with one dollar (100¢). How much money will you get back?

TICKET PRICES	
Main Street	38¢
Lincoln Street	46¢
Pleasant Street	57¢
Green Street	63¢
Spring Street	75¢
Newton Street	82¢

I pay with one dollar.

My change is _____.

I pay with one dollar.

My change is _____.

I pay with one dollar.

My change is _____.

I pay with one dollar.

My change is _____.

Story Problems with Unknown Partners

Name _____

Homework

Solve each story problem. **Show your work.**

---

1. Alma has 129 stars to make a poster. Larry has 82 stars. How many fewer stars does Larry have than Alma?

[_____] _____
                    label

---

2. The library had 61 magazines. Today they got new magazines. Now there are 135 magazines. How many new magazines did the library get?

[_____] _____
                    label

---

3. Mori put 209 pretzels in a bowl for her party. Her friends ate some. Now there are 72 pretzels. How many pretzels did her friends eat?

[_____] _____
                    label

---

4. Eric's hockey team scored 41 goals, and Lou's team scored 110 goals. How many more goals did Lou's team score than Eric's team?

[_____] _____
                    label

Name _____

Remembering

Solve the story problem.   **Show your work.**

I. Al made 163 pickles for the Perfect
Pickle contest. The judges ate 74 of
them. How many of Al's pickles
are left?

_____
label

---

2. Complete the bar graph using the information below.

- Alicia has 5 chores to do.
- Kim has 4 more chores than Alicia.
- Roberto has to finish 2 more chores to have as
  many chores as Alicia.
- Tyrone has 2 fewer chores than Roberto.

Household Chores

Add.

3. 100 + 83 = _____   **4.** 100 + 6 = _____

  10 + 83 = _____   10 + 6 = _____

   1 + 83 = _____   1 + 6 = _____

True or False? Ring the answer. Then give 3 examples for a true statement or one example for a false statement.

1. If the midpoints of the sides of a quadrilateral are connected with four straight lines, four quadrilaterals will be formed.

True   False

2. If you add the digits in a 3s count-by, the total will be 3, 6, or 9.

True   False

_____
_____
_____

3. If the midpoints of the sides of a triangle are connected with three straight lines, three triangles will be formed.

True   False

4. If you add two even numbers, the total will be odd.

True   False

_____
_____
_____

5. Write a false statement and an example to show it is false.

_____
_____
_____
_____
_____

|

Remembering

Solve each story problem.   **Show your work.**

1. Mr. Lopez had 135 puppets in his toy store. He sold 48 puppets. How many puppets does he have left?

puppets

[   ] _____
       label

2. Mary has 36 dog stamps and 47 cat stamps. Tam has 142 dog stamps and 56 cat stamps. How many dog stamps do they have all together?

dog stamps

[   ] _____
       label

Find all possible answers.

3. Pedro is thinking of a number. The number has 3 digits. The digit in the hundreds place is 6 more than the digit in the tens place. The digit in the ones place is 4. What number could Pedro be thinking of? _____

4. Ming-Na is thinking of a number. The number is between 30 and 40. It is an even number. The digit in the tens place is less than the digit in the ones place. What number could Ming-Na be thinking of? _____

Use Mathematical Processes

Homework

Name _____

1. Which two figures are congruent?

Figures _____ and _____ are congruent.

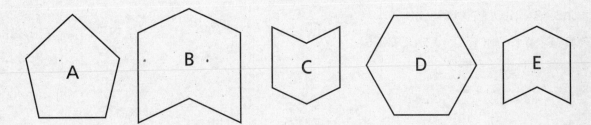

Are the two figures similar? Write *similar* or *not similar*.

2.   **3.**   **4.**

_____   _____   _____

5. Sort these shapes into two groups using your own rule.

My sorting rule is _____.

Figures _____ are _____.

Figures _____ are _____.

6. On the Back Draw six polygons. Label each with a letter.
Describe a sorting rule and sort the figures according to your rule.

Compare Shapes

Name _____

Homework

Cut out the pattern blocks from page M58.
Use them to complete the exercises.

1. Combine shapes to show 2 ways to make a trapezoid.
   List the shapes you used and how many.

   _____

   _____

2. Combine shapes to show 3 ways to make a hexagon.
   List the shapes you used and how many.

   _____

   _____

   _____

Ring the shapes you can cut to make the named shapes.
Cut them to check.

3. 2 triangles

4. 4 squares

5. **On the Back** Draw 3 different shapes. Draw a shape you can make by combining the 3 shapes.

Combine and Cut Shapes

Name _____

Homework

Write *slide, flip,* or *turn* to describe how the figure moved.

1.

_____

2.

_____

3.

P | ꟼ

_____

4.

꒒ P

_____

Draw the next figure in the pattern.

5.
   _____

6.
   _____

⟶ **7. On the Back** Find a flat object in your home and trace it. Slide it to the left and trace it again. Then show a turn using the same object.

Name _____

Motion Geometry

Homework

Draw what comes next in each pattern.

1. ◯ ◯ ■ ◯ ◯ ■ ◯ ◯ ■ ____

2.

3.

4.

____

5. Draw and cut out a letter. Trace it to show a motion pattern.

6. On the Back Draw a growing pattern.

Patterns with Shapes

Name _____

Homework

Find the area of each shaded figure in square centimeters.

1.

Area = ☐ square centimeters

2.

Area = ☐ square centimeters

3.

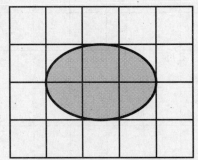

Area = ☐ square centimeters

4.

Area = ☐ square centimeters

Estimate the area of each figure in square centimeters.

5.

Estimate of area:

☐ square centimeters

6.

Estimate of area:

☐ square centimeters

7. On the Back Draw three different figures and estimate the area of each in square centimeters.

Name

Count Square Units

Homework

Count the hundreds, tens, and ones.
Write the totals.

1. ☐ ||||| |||| ⚬⚬⚬⚬⚬ ⚬⚬⚬

_____ _____ _____   Total _____
Hundreds   Tens   Ones

2. ☐☐ ||||| ⚬⚬⚬⚬⚬
   ☐☐   ⚬⚬⚬⚬

_____ _____ _____   Total _____
Hundreds   Tens   Ones

Draw the hundreds, tens, and ones for the
numbers below. Use boxes, sticks, and circles.

3. ___2___   ___4___   ___3___ | 4. ___5___   ___6___   ___8___
   Hundreds   Tens   Ones | Hundreds   Tens   Ones

5. ___3___   ___8___   ___2___ | 6. ___1___   ___7___   ___7___
   Hundreds   Tens   Ones | Hundreds   Tens   Ones

Name _____

Targeted Practice

Add or subtract.

1. $\begin{array}{r} 164 \\ -\ 53 \\ \hline \end{array}$

2. $\begin{array}{r} 136 \\ +\ 73 \\ \hline \end{array}$

3. $\begin{array}{r} 150 \\ -\ 65 \\ \hline \end{array}$

4. $\begin{array}{r} 145 \\ +\ 83 \\ \hline \end{array}$

5. $\begin{array}{r} 107 \\ -\ 44 \\ \hline \end{array}$

6. $\begin{array}{r} 138 \\ +\ 56 \\ \hline \end{array}$

7. $\begin{array}{r} 160 \\ -\ 42 \\ \hline \end{array}$

8. $\begin{array}{r} 123 \\ +\ 61 \\ \hline \end{array}$

9. $\begin{array}{r} 114 \\ -\ 72 \\ \hline \end{array}$

10. $\begin{array}{r} 187 \\ +\ 93 \\ \hline \end{array}$

11. $\begin{array}{r} 109 \\ -\ 88 \\ \hline \end{array}$

12. $\begin{array}{r} 175 \\ +\ 94 \\ \hline \end{array}$

Count Numbers to 1,000

Name _____

Write the hundreds, tens, and ones.

1. $675 = \underline{600} + \underline{70} + \underline{5}$
   H T O

2. $519 = \underline{\hspace{1cm}} + \underline{\hspace{1cm}} + \underline{\hspace{1cm}}$

3. $831 = \underline{\hspace{1cm}} + \underline{\hspace{1cm}} + \underline{\hspace{1cm}}$

4. $487 = \underline{\hspace{1cm}} + \underline{\hspace{1cm}} + \underline{\hspace{1cm}}$

5. $222 = \underline{\hspace{1cm}} + \underline{\hspace{1cm}} + \underline{\hspace{1cm}}$

6. $765 = \underline{\hspace{1cm}} + \underline{\hspace{1cm}} + \underline{\hspace{1cm}}$

Write the number.

7. $300 + 40 + 6 = \underline{3\ 4\ 6}$
   H T O

8. $100 + 60 + 2 = \underline{\hspace{1.5cm}}$

9. $700 + 20 + 4 = \underline{\hspace{1.5cm}}$

10. $200 + 50 + 3 = \underline{\hspace{1.5cm}}$

11. $400 + 70 + 1 = \underline{\hspace{1.5cm}}$

12. $800 + 80 + 8 = \underline{\hspace{1.5cm}}$

Write the missing number. Watch the hundreds,
tens, and ones. They are out of order.

13. $\underline{\hspace{1.5cm}} = 30 + 5 + 400$

14. $2 + 80 + 600 = \underline{\hspace{1.5cm}}$

15. $\underline{\hspace{1.5cm}} = 60 + 800 + 3$

16. $900 + 7 + 40 = \underline{\hspace{1.5cm}}$

17. $\underline{\hspace{1.5cm}} = 300 + 4 + 50$

18. $1 + 500 + 70 = \underline{\hspace{1.5cm}}$

19. $729 = 20 + 9 + \underline{\hspace{1.5cm}}$

20. $\underline{\hspace{1.5cm}} + 6 + 200 = 296$

Name _____

Remembering

Complete the number sequence. Write the rule.

1. 43, 39, 35, _____, _____, _____ Rule: n _____

2. 66, 69, 72, _____, _____, _____ Rule: n _____

Write the hundreds, tens, and ones. | Write the number.

3. 695 = ____ + ____ + ____   5. 400 + 30 + 6 = ____

4. 547 = ____ + ____ + ____   6. 700 + 80 + 1 = ____

Add ones, tens, or a hundred.

7. 100 + 58 = ____   8. 3 + 100 = ____

    10 + 58 = ____   3 + 10 = ____

     1 + 58 = ____   3 + 1 = ____

Add or subtract.

9.   126
   − 59
   ‾‾‾‾‾

10.   93
    − 45
    ‾‾‾‾‾

11.   78
    + 67
    ‾‾‾‾‾

12. **Time** On a separate sheet of paper, draw what you do at 8 o'clock in the morning. Show the time on a digital clock.

         Place Value

Homework

Count by ones. Write the numbers.

1. 396 397 _398_ _399_ _400_ _401_ _402_ _403_ _404_ _405_ 406

2. 695 696 ___ ___ ___ ___ ___ ___ ___ ___ 705

3. 498 499 ___ ___ ___ ___ ___ ___ ___ ___ 508

4. 894 ___ ___ ___ ___ ___ ___ ___ ___ ___ 904

5. 796 ___ ___ ___ ___ ___ ___ ___ ___ ___ 806

6. 597 ___ ___ ___ ___ ___ ___ ___ ___ ___ 607

Count by tens. Write the numbers.

7. 830 840 _850_ _860_ _870_ _880_ _890_ _900_ _910_ _920_ 930

8. 470 480 ___ ___ ___ ___ ___ ___ ___ ___ 570

9. 740 ___ ___ ___ ___ ___ ___ ___ ___ ___ 840

10. 380 ___ ___ ___ ___ ___ ___ ___ ___ ___ 480

11. 560 ___ ___ ___ ___ ___ ___ ___ ___ ___ 660

12. 690 ___ ___ ___ ___ ___ ___ ___ ___ ___ 790

Name _____

Targeted Practice

Subtract.

1. $\begin{array}{r} 110 \\ -47 \\ \hline \end{array}$

2. $\begin{array}{r} 190 \\ -95 \\ \hline \end{array}$

3. $\begin{array}{r} 106 \\ -59 \\ \hline \end{array}$

4. $\begin{array}{r} 107 \\ -68 \\ \hline \end{array}$

5. $\begin{array}{r} 160 \\ -74 \\ \hline \end{array}$

6. $\begin{array}{r} 102 \\ -36 \\ \hline \end{array}$

7. $\begin{array}{r} 140 \\ -68 \\ \hline \end{array}$

8. $\begin{array}{r} 105 \\ -23 \\ \hline \end{array}$

9. $\begin{array}{r} 130 \\ -52 \\ \hline \end{array}$

10. $\begin{array}{r} 103 \\ -98 \\ \hline \end{array}$

11. $\begin{array}{r} 108 \\ -84 \\ \hline \end{array}$

12. $\begin{array}{r} 150 \\ -64 \\ \hline \end{array}$

Count by Ones and by Tens

Homework

Add or subtract.

1. $\begin{array}{r} 46 \\ + 97 \\ \hline \end{array}$

2. $\begin{array}{r} 154 \\ - 83 \\ \hline \end{array}$

3. $\begin{array}{r} 74 \\ + 58 \\ \hline \end{array}$

Solve each story problem.   **Show your work.**

4. You have 100¢ to buy a necklace.
   The necklace costs 67¢. How much
   change should you get back?

   ☐ ¢

5. Joy caught 47 insects. Ben caught
   56. How many insects did the two
   children catch altogether?

   ☐ _____
        label

6. What number is shown?

7. Draw boxes, sticks, and circles to
   show the number 348.

_____

Name _____

Remembering

Under the coins, write the total amount of money so far.

I.

___ ___ ___ ___ ___ ___ ___

Use the table to answer the questions.
Fill in the boxes with numbers.
Ring *more* or *fewer*.

Toys

	Toy Trucks	Toy Cars
Molly	85	49
Jake	68	57

2. Jake has [ ] *more* *fewer* toy trucks than Molly has.

3. Molly has [ ] *more* *fewer* toy cars than Jake has.

4. The children have [ ] toy trucks altogether.

Count by ones.

5. 793 _794_ ___ ___ ___ ___ ___ ___ ___ ___ 803

Count by tens.

6. 840 _850_ ___ ___ ___ ___ ___ ___ ___ ___ 940

7. **Time** On a separate sheet of paper, draw what you do at
9 o'clock in the morning. Draw a clock face and
show the time.

Group into Hundreds

Name _____

Homework

Solve each story problem.

1. Maria blew up some balloons for a party. She divided them into 4 groups of one hundred and 7 groups of ten. 6 balloons were left over. How many balloons did Maria blow up for the party?

   [   ] _____
           label

2. Roger has 5 erasers. He bought 6 packages of one hundred and 2 packages of ten. How many erasers does Roger have altogether?

   [   ] _____
           label

3. Add.

$400 + 200 =$ _____ $440 + 7 =$ _____ $16 + 700 =$ _____

$40 + 50 =$ _____ $84 + 10 =$ _____ $70 + 7 =$ _____

$8 + 460 =$ _____ $200 + 9 =$ _____ $53 + 500 =$ _____

$30 + 10 =$ _____ $60 + 40 =$ _____ $60 + 4 =$ _____

$380 + 10 =$ _____ $900 + 80 =$ _____ $800 + 200 =$ _____

Targeted Practice

Count by ones. Write the numbers.

1. 399 400 _401_ _402_ _403_ _404_ _405_ _406_ _407_ _408_ 409

2. 596 597 ___ ___ ___ ___ ___ ___ ___ ___ 606

3. 498 499 ___ ___ ___ ___ ___ ___ ___ ___ 508

4. 794 ___ ___ ___ ___ ___ ___ ___ ___ ___ 804

5. 891 ___ ___ ___ ___ ___ ___ ___ ___ ___ 901

6. 597 ___ ___ ___ ___ ___ ___ ___ ___ ___ 607

Count by tens. Write the numbers.

7. 330 340 _350_ _360_ _370_ _380_ _390_ _400_ _410_ _420_ 430

8. 680 690 ___ ___ ___ ___ ___ ___ ___ ___ 780

9. 820 ___ ___ ___ ___ ___ ___ ___ ___ ___ 920

10. 470 ___ ___ ___ ___ ___ ___ ___ ___ ___ 570

11. 760 ___ ___ ___ ___ ___ ___ ___ ___ ___ 860

12. 690 ___ ___ ___ ___ ___ ___ ___ ___ ___ 790

Add Ones, Tens, and Hundreds

Name _____

Homework

The quarter machine is broken today. Sometimes it works. Sometimes it doesn't. Write "Yes" if it gave you 25¢. Write "No" if it didn't.

10¢   1¢   5¢

1. Quarter Machine →

25¢? _____

2. Quarter Machine →

25¢? _____

3. Quarter Machine →

25¢? _____

4. Quarter Machine →

25¢? _____

Name _____

Remembering

Add or subtract.

1.
```
   8 1
 + 6 7
```
```
   5 8
 + 2 5
```
```
  1 6 7
 -  7 8
```

Find the unknown partner.

2.

Continue the number sequence.

3. 48, 54, 60 ____, ____, ____, ____, ____   Rule: n _____

4. 55, 52, 49 ____, ____, ____, ____, ____   Rule: n _____

Solve.

5. The bakery had fresh dinner rolls. They counted 5 boxes of one hundred rolls and 8 boxes of ten rolls. They had 3 more rolls. How many rolls did the bakery have?

6. Noah collects baseball cards. He has 2 boxes of one hundred cards and 4 boxes of ten cards. He also has 9 loose cards. How many cards does Noah have in total?

```
┌──────┐
│      │  _____
└──────┘    label
```

```
┌──────┐
│      │  _____
└──────┘    label
```

Review Quarters

Name _____

Homework

Rewrite these money amounts.

1. 152¢ = $1.52   2. $4.86 = 486¢   3. $0.06 = _____

   36¢ = _____   273¢ = _____   5¢ = _____

   $5.03 = _____ $4.57 = _____ $3.20 = _____

Count by ones.

4. 26 ___ ___ ___ ___ ___ ___ ___ ___ ___ 36

5. 597 ___ ___ ___ ___ ___ ___ ___ ___ ___ 607

Count by tens.

6. 220 ___ ___ ___ ___ ___ ___ ___ ___ ___ 320

7. 830 ___ ___ ___ ___ ___ ___ ___ ___ ___ 930

Add.

8. $3.96 + $0.08 = $ ___ · ___   9. $0.09 + $6.93 = $ ___ · ___

   3¢ + 798¢ =   _____¢   196¢ + 6¢ =   _____¢

   $5.97 + $0.05 = $ ___ · ___ $0.07 + $2.99 = $ ___ · ___

   494¢ + 9¢ =   _____¢   894¢ + 8¢ =   _____¢

Name _____

Targeted Practice

Count by ones. Write the numbers.

1. 596 597 <u>598</u> <u>599</u> <u>600</u> <u>601</u> <u>602</u> <u>603</u> <u>604</u> <u>605</u> 606

2. 592 593 ___ ___ ___ ___ ___ ___ ___ ___ 602

3. 895 896 ___ ___ ___ ___ ___ ___ ___ ___ 905

4. 799 ___ ___ ___ ___ ___ ___ ___ ___ ___ 809

5. 491 ___ ___ ___ ___ ___ ___ ___ ___ ___ 501

6. 695 ___ ___ ___ ___ ___ ___ ___ ___ ___ 705

Count by tens. Write the numbers.

7. 630 640 <u>650</u> <u>660</u> <u>670</u> <u>680</u> <u>690</u> <u>700</u> <u>710</u> <u>720</u> 730

8. 870 880 ___ ___ ___ ___ ___ ___ ___ ___ 970

9. 790 ___ ___ ___ ___ ___ ___ ___ ___ ___ 890

10. 380 ___ ___ ___ ___ ___ ___ ___ ___ ___ 480

11. 550 ___ ___ ___ ___ ___ ___ ___ ___ ___ 650

12. 460 ___ ___ ___ ___ ___ ___ ___ ___ ___ 560

Buy with Dollars and Cents

Name _____

Homework

Here are some foods from the Grocery Store. The prices are shown too. Answer the questions below.

10 Hot Dogs $2.49	4 Granola Bars $4.25	8 Ears of Corn $1.58
1 Dozen Yogurts $3.22	2 Bunches of Grapes $0.98	5 Jars of Pickles $2.13

How much change would you get from $5.00 if you bought

1. 10 hot dogs?

$ 2.51

$$\begin{array}{r} \overset{9}{\cancel{4}}\ \overset{10}{\cancel{10}}\ 10 \\ \$\cancel{5}.\cancel{0}\cancel{0} \\ -\ 2.49 \\ \hline \$2.51 \end{array} \quad \text{or} \quad \begin{array}{r} 4\ 9\ 10 \\ \$5.00 \\ -\ 2.49 \\ \hline \$2.51 \end{array}$$

2. 2 bunches of grapes? $ ___ . ___

3. 8 ears of corn? $ ___ . ___

4. 5 jars of pickles? $ ___ . ___

5. 1 dozen yogurts? $ ___ . ___

6. 4 granola bars? $ ___ . ___

Name _____

Remembering

Use the information in the table to answer
the questions.

1. Altogether, how many tuna
   and turkey sandwiches
   were sold?

   _____

Sandwiches Sold at the Ballpark

Sandwich	Number Sold
Tuna	18
Peanut Butter	57
Ham	39
Chicken	83
Turkey	26

2. Which three kinds of sandwiches
   together had the same number
   sold as chicken?

   _____ ,

   _____ , and

   _____ .

3. How many more turkey sandwiches need to be
   sold to equal the number of ham

   sandwiches sold? _____

4. How many more ham sandwiches need to be
   sold to equal the number of peanut butter

   sandwiches sold? _____

5. How many fewer chicken sandwiches would
   have to be sold to equal the number of tuna

   sandwiches sold? _____

6. How many fewer chicken sandwiches would
   have to be sold to equal the number of turkey

   sandwiches sold? _____

Change from $5.00

Name _____

Homework

Solve each story problem.

1. Rita counts the visitors to the museum. She counted 5 groups of one hundred and 2 groups of ten. She also counted a small group of 7. How many visitors did Rita count?

2. Kay packs buttons at the button factory. She packed 7 boxes of one hundred buttons and 5 boxes of ten. She packed one box of 9 buttons. How many buttons did Kay pack?

```
┌─────────┐
│         │      _____
└─────────┘            label
```

```
┌─────────┐
│         │      _____
└─────────┘            label
```

Add.

3. $297 + 3 =$ _____

$7 + 285 =$ _____

$5 + 143 =$ _____

$100 + 200 =$ _____

4. $98 + 9 =$ _____

$6 + 97 =$ _____

$45 + 3 =$ _____

$40 + 30 =$ _____

5. $38 + 500 =$ _____

$9 + 300 =$ _____

$295 + 9 =$ _____

$50 + 500 =$ _____

6. $200 + 200 =$ _____

$11 + 80 =$ _____

$30 + 410 =$ _____

$20 + 380 =$ _____

Targeted Practice

Add or subtract.

1. $\begin{array}{r} 200 \\ -\ 79 \\ \hline \end{array}$
2. $\begin{array}{r} 100 \\ -\ 48 \\ \hline \end{array}$
3. $\begin{array}{r} 200 \\ -\ 87 \\ \hline \end{array}$

4. $\begin{array}{r} 100 \\ -\ 35 \\ \hline \end{array}$
5. $\begin{array}{r} 200 \\ -\ 51 \\ \hline \end{array}$
6. $\begin{array}{r} 100 \\ -\ 62 \\ \hline \end{array}$

7. $\begin{array}{r} 200 \\ +116 \\ \hline \end{array}$
8. $\begin{array}{r} 100 \\ +324 \\ \hline \end{array}$
9. $\begin{array}{r} 200 \\ +597 \\ \hline \end{array}$

10. $\begin{array}{r} 100 \\ +243 \\ \hline \end{array}$
11. $\begin{array}{r} 200 \\ +458 \\ \hline \end{array}$
12. $\begin{array}{r} 100 \\ +677 \\ \hline \end{array}$

Homework

Solve each story problem.

1. Martin sold 58 tickets to the roller coaster ride. He sold 267 tickets to the boat ride. How many tickets did Martin sell?

2. Justine jumped 485 times on a pogo stick. Then she jumped 329 times when she tried again. How many times did she jump altogether?

[   ] _____   [   ] _____
         label   label

Add.

3. $18 + 549 =$ [   ]

4. $190 + 89 =$ [   ]

5. $76 + 570 =$ [   ]

6. $75 + 656 =$ [   ]

7. $348 + 162 =$ [   ]

8. $407 + 394 =$ [   ]

Name _____

Remembering

Complete the number sequence. Write the rule.

1. 84, 86, 88, _____, _____, _____   Rule: *n* _____

2. 52, 46, 40, _____, _____, _____   Rule: *n* _____

3. 21, 29, 37, _____, _____, _____   Rule: *n* _____

How much money is shown here?

4. = _____ ¢

5. = _____ ¢

Find each unknown partner.

6.   7.   8.

Solve the story problem.   **Show your work.**

9. The library has 180 CDs in its collection. One morning 28 CDs were checked out. In the afternoon 56 CDs were checked out. How many CDs were not checked out?

☐ _____
   label

Solve and Discuss

Homework

Add. Use any method.

1. $2.67
    + $1.56

    Make a new ten? _____

    Make a new hundred? _____

2. $4.82
    + $3.43

    Make a new ten? _____

    Make a new hundred? _____

3. $2.75
    + $5.39

    Make a new ten? _____

    Make a new hundred? _____

4. $6.09
    + $1.88

    Make a new ten? _____

    Make a new hundred? _____

5. $2.94
    + $4.12

    Make a new ten? _____

    Make a new hundred? _____

6. $3.07
    + $3.66

    Make a new ten? _____

    Make a new hundred? _____

Name _____

Targeted Practice

Solve the story problems.

1. Penny has 596 umbrellas in her store. Kamala has 235 umbrellas in her store. How many umbrellas are in both stores?

```
┌──────────┐
│          │  _____
└──────────┘     label
```

2. There are 387 rulers in a box. Yesterday, Milo put 113 more rulers in the box. How many rulers are in the box now?

```
┌──────────┐
│          │  _____
└──────────┘     label
```

3. There are 249 ants crawling up a tree. There are 373 ants on an ant hill. How many ants are there in all?

```
┌──────────┐
│          │  _____
└──────────┘     label
```

4. Stephanie collected 648 pieces of fabric for a huge quilt. Today, Stephanie added 261 pieces. How many pieces does she have in all?

```
┌──────────┐
│          │  _____
└──────────┘     label
```

Add Money Amounts

Homework

Name _____

Add. Use any method.

1.   4 5 9
   + 2 6 7

Make a new ten? _____

Make a new hundred? _____

2. 1 8 7 + 3 7 4 = _____

Make a new ten? _____

Make a new hundred? _____

3.   6 7 8
   +   1 5

Make a new ten? _____

Make a new hundred? _____

4. 6 3 5 + 9 2 = _____

Make a new ten? _____

Make a new hundred? _____

5.   3 8 9
   + 5 4 9

Make a new ten? _____

Make a new hundred? _____

6. 6 4 + 8 9 7 = _____

Make a new ten? _____

Make a new hundred? _____

Remembering

Find each unknown partner.

1.

2.

3.

Rewrite the money amount. The first one is done for you.

4. 528¢ = $ <u>5.28</u>

   62¢ = $ <u>0.62</u>

  $.07 = <u> 7 </u> ¢

5. $1.10 = _____ ¢

   8¢ = $ _____

  $4.90 = _____ ¢

Count by tens.

6. 540 ___ ___ ___ ___ ___ ___ ___ ___ ___ 640

7. 620 ___ ___ ___ ___ ___ ___ ___ ___ ___ 720

Add.

8. $4.98 + $0.05 = $_____

    5¢ + 799¢ = _____ ¢

  $6.97 + $0.09 = $_____

   895¢ + 7¢ = _____ ¢

9. $0.07 + $5.94 = $_____

   292¢ + 9¢ = _____ ¢

  $0.06 + $3.96 = $_____

   193¢ + 8¢ = _____ ¢

Homework

Add. Use any method.

1.
$$\begin{array}{r} 114 \\ +286 \\ \hline \end{array}$$

Make a new ten? _____

Make a new hundred? _____

2.
$$\begin{array}{r} 207 \\ +595 \\ \hline \end{array}$$

Make a new ten? _____

Make a new hundred? _____

3. $68 + 393 =$ _____

Make a new ten? _____

Make a new hundred? _____

4. $457 + 72 =$ _____

Make a new ten? _____

Make a new hundred? _____

5.
$$\begin{array}{r} 328 \\ +235 \\ \hline \end{array}$$

Make a new ten? _____

Make a new hundred? _____

6.
$$\begin{array}{r} 549 \\ +326 \\ \hline \end{array}$$

Make a new ten? _____

Make a new hundred? _____

Name _____

Targeted Practice

Add.

1. 176
   +217

2. 347
   +242

3. 514
   +367

4. 368
   +624

5. 224
   +374

6. 533
   +156

7. 427
   +257

8. 314
   +569

9. 348
   +239

10. 485
   +214

11. 124
   +566

12. 354
   +218

Story Problems: Unknown Addends

Homework

Solve the story problems. Use your favorite method.
Make a Proof Drawing if it helps.

1. Ricardo likes olives. He had 100 olives. He ate 43 of them. How many olives does he have left?

[ ] _____
label

2. Dawn has 300 pennies in her piggy bank. She gave some to her sister. Now she has 147 left. How many pennies did Dawn give to her sister?

[ ] _____
label

3. Tory sells hockey sticks to teams in her city. She had 500 and sold 353 to one team. How many hockey sticks does she have left to sell?

[ ] _____
label

4. Randy collects magnets. Over two years he collected 400 magnets. He collected 125 magnets the first year. How many did he collect the second year?

[ ] _____
label

Name _____

Remembering

Continue the number sequence.

I. 88, 93, 98 ____, ____, ____, ____, ____   Rule: *n* _____

67, 64, 61 ____, ____, ____, ____, ____   Rule: *n* _____

Add.

2. $6.92 + $0.19 = $_____   **3.** $0.07 + $2.98 = $_____

14¢ + 388¢ = _____ ¢   193¢ + 8¢ = _____ ¢

Write the hundreds, tens, and ones. | Write the number.

4. 837 = ____ + ____ + ____   **5.** 300 + 40 + 8 = _____

902 = ____ + ____ + ____   500 + 20 + 0 = _____

Count by tens.

6. 420 ___ ___ ___ ___ ___ ___ ___ ___ ___ 520

7. 650 ___ ___ ___ ___ ___ ___ ___ ___ ___ 750

Find each unknown partner.

8.

100   100   100

22 ☐   79 ☐   87 ☐

Story Problems with Hundreds Numbers

Homework

Decide if you need to ungroup. If you need to ungroup, draw a magnifying glass around the top number. Then find the answer.

1. $$\begin{array}{r} 730 \\ -499 \\ \hline \end{array}$$

Ungroup to get 10 ones? _____

Ungroup to get 10 tens? _____

2. $$\begin{array}{r} 950 \\ -639 \\ \hline \end{array}$$

Ungroup to get 10 ones? _____

Ungroup to get 10 tens? _____

3. $$\begin{array}{r} 300 \\ -167 \\ \hline \end{array}$$

Ungroup to get 10 ones? _____

Ungroup to get 10 tens? _____

4. $$\begin{array}{r} 404 \\ -188 \\ \hline \end{array}$$

Ungroup to get 10 ones? _____

Ungroup to get 10 tens? _____

5. $$\begin{array}{r} 420 \\ -183 \\ \hline \end{array}$$

Ungroup to get 10 ones? _____

Ungroup to get 10 tens? _____

6. $502 - 149 =$ _____

Ungroup to get 10 ones? _____

Ungroup to get 10 tens? _____

Name _____

Targeted Practice

Add.

1. 226
    + 457

2. 547
    + 332

3. 424
    + 357

4. 458
    + 214

5. 114
    + 874

6. 623
    + 256

7. 537
    + 457

8. 424
    + 269

9. 458
    + 439

10. 575
    + 324

11. 234
    + 456

12. 438
    + 329

Subtract from Numbers with Zeros

Name _____

Homework

Decide if you need to ungroup. If you need to ungroup,
draw a magnifying glass around the top number. Then find
the answer.

1. $4.0 8
   - $0.5 3
   _____

   Ungroup to get 10 ones? _____

   Ungroup to get 10 tens? _____

2. $7.1 0
   - $2.2 8
   _____

   Ungroup to get 10 ones? _____

   Ungroup to get 10 tens? _____

3. $3.0 0
   - $2.6 8
   _____

   Ungroup to get 10 ones? _____

   Ungroup to get 10 tens? _____

4. $2.0 7
   - $0.5 5
   _____

   Ungroup to get 10 ones? _____

   Ungroup to get 10 tens? _____

5. $5.9 0
   - $1.7 7
   _____

   Ungroup to get 10 ones? _____

   Ungroup to get 10 tens? _____

6. $9.0 3
   - $6.3 3
   _____

   Ungroup to get 10 ones? _____

   Ungroup to get 10 tens? _____

Name _____

Remembering

How much money is shown here?

1. = _____ ¢

39¢ 75

Add or subtract.

2. 375
   +246

3. 546
   +262

4. 151
   − 82

5. 118
   − 65

Complete the number sequence. Write the rule.

6. 11, 17, 23, _____, _____, _____   Rule: *n* _____

Write 8 equations for the Math Mountain.

7. 223

   91   132

   _____   _____

   _____   _____

   _____   _____

   _____

Subtract.

8. 400
   − 34

9. 630
   − 59

10. 701
    − 93

11. 226
    − 37

Subtract Money Amounts

Name _____

Homework

Decide if you need to ungroup. If you need to ungroup, draw
a magnifying glass around the top number. Then find the answer.

1.
```
   5 3 1
 - 4 3 4
 ───────
```

Ungroup to get 10 ones? _____

Ungroup to get 10 tens? _____

2.
```
   5 7 9
 - 2 9 6
 ───────
```

Ungroup to get 10 ones? _____

Ungroup to get 10 tens? _____

3.
```
   3 9 1
 - 2 6 5
 ───────
```

Ungroup to get 10 ones? _____

Ungroup to get 10 tens? _____

4. 238 − 177 = _____

Ungroup to get 10 ones? _____

Ungroup to get 10 tens? _____

5. Latoya plans to drive 572 miles
on her vacation. The first day
she drove 386 miles. How many
more miles does she have to
drive?

6. Elena had $7.35. She bought a
gift for $4.27. How much money
does she have left?

label

Targeted Practice

Solve each story problem.

1. Carrie has 654 stamps in her stamp collection. Hector has 327 stamps in his collection. How many stamps are there in both collections?

[ ] _____
         label

2. In one week, Farida drove her motorcycle 569 miles. The next week she drove 253 miles. How many miles did she drive in the two weeks?

[ ] _____
         label

3. Kuri has read 369 pages in her book. This weekend, Kuri plans to read 252 pages. How many pages will Kuri have read at the end of this weekend?

[ ] _____
         label

4. Armani has saved up 283 dollars. Lita has saved up 327 dollars. How much money do Armani and Lita have together?

[ ] _____
         label

Subtract from Any 3-Digit Number

Homework

Decide if you need to ungroup. If you need to ungroup,
draw a magnifying glass around the top number. Then find
the answer.

1. 6 3 0
   − 3 1 8
   ─────────

Ungroup to get 10 ones? _____

Ungroup to get 10 tens? _____

2. 9 3 1
   − 8 4 5
   ─────────

Ungroup to get 10 ones? _____

Ungroup to get 10 tens? _____

3. 4 0 7
   − 2 7 4
   ─────────

Ungroup to get 10 ones? _____

Ungroup to get 10 tens? _____

4. 4 9 8
   − 2 7 6
   ─────────

Ungroup to get 10 ones? _____

Ungroup to get 10 tens? _____

5. Jamal had 590 craft sticks. He
   used 413 craft sticks to make a
   building. How many craft sticks
   does he have left?

6. Clare and her family are driving
   to Blue Valley Mountains. Blue
   Valley Mountains is 290 miles
   from their home. They drove
   184 miles. How many more
   miles do they have to go?

☐ _____
       label

☐ _____
       label

Remembering

Complete the money tables.

1.

49¢	
Q	
D	I
N	
P	

= ¢
= 10¢
= ¢
= ¢
¢

2.

72¢	
Q	2
D	
N	
P	2

= 50¢
= ¢
= ¢
= ¢
¢

3.

65¢	
Q	
D	
N	
P	0

= ¢
= ¢
= ¢
= 0¢
¢

The market sells fresh fruit. The table shows how much fruit they sold this week.

Fresh Fruit Sold This Week

Lemons	200
Apples	680
Bananas	450

4. How many fewer lemons did the market sell than bananas?

_____

5. How many more apples did the market sell than bananas?

_____

6. How many fewer lemons did the market sell than apples?

_____

7. Time On a separate piece of paper, draw what you do at 10 o'clock P.M. Show the time on a digital clock.

Practice Ungrouping

Homework

Decide if you need to add or subtract. Then solve
each problem.

1.   1 8 4
 + 4 3 3

2.   5 5 2
 − 3 9 9

3.   3 2 8
 − 1 1 9

4.   2 8 8
 + 2 9 4

5. 967 − 548 = _____

6. 474 − 355 = _____

Name _____

Targeted Practice

Subtract.

1.   391
      −265
      ——————

2.   648
      −156
      ——————

3.   925
      −583
      ——————

4.   362
      −171
      ——————

5.   652
      −234
      ——————

6.   774
      −258
      ——————

Relationships between Addition and Subtraction Methods

Homework

Solve each story problem.

1. Abigail's mother gave her some carrots to sell at the state fair. Then Abigail picked 367 more from the garden. Now Abigail has 825 carrots to sell. How many did her mother give her?

[ ] _____
label

2. Stanley the grocer had lots of mushrooms. He sold 679 in the morning. Now he has 244 left to sell. How many mushrooms did Stanley have at the beginning?

[ ] _____
label

3. Carmen has 347 guppies in her fish tank. Peter must give away 156 of his guppies to have the same number as Carmen. How many guppies does Peter have in his tank?

[ ] _____
label

4. Stanley bought 283 bags of flour for his store. Ted needs 148 bags of flour to have as many as Stanley. How many bags of flour does Ted have?

[ ] _____
label

Name _____

Remembering

Add or subtract.

1.
```
  5 0 4        9 6 2        $4.7 3
+ 3 9 9      - 7 7 5      - $2.5 8
```

Write the hundreds, tens, and ones.

2. 382 = _____ + _____ + _____

   738 = _____ + _____ + _____

Write the number.

3. 90 + 0 + 400 = _____

   6 + 500 + 10 = _____

Solve each story problem.

4. 198 people are already on an airplane. The rest are waiting to get on. There are 347 people altogether. How many people are waiting to get on the airplane?

   [ ] _____
   label

5. Colby is practicing football. He kicked the ball 168 times this morning. He kicked the ball 207 times this afternoon. How many times did he kick today?

   [ ] _____
   label

6. **Time** On a separate piece of paper, draw what you do at 6 o'clock in the morning. Draw a clock face and show the time.

Unknown Start and Comparison Problems

Name _____

Homework

Solve each story problem.

1. Mario bought 644 plastic cups. He gave 337 to the art teacher. How many cups did he have left?

[   ] _____
     label

2. Joel collects baseball cards. He had 568 cards. Then he bought 329 more at a yard sale. How many cards does he have now?

[   ] _____
     label

3. A bird collected 392 sticks to build a nest. Then she collected 165 more. How many sticks did the bird collect?

[   ] _____
     label

4. There are 765 books in the school library. 259 are paperback, and the rest are hardcover. How many hardcover books are there in the library?

[   ] _____
     label

Name _____

Targeted Practice

Solve each story problem.

1. Some children had 458 raisins. They got hungry and ate some of them. Now they have 285 left. How many raisins did they eat?

   ![box] _____
   label

2. Tom collects rocks. Last night, he went to the beach and found 329 rocks. This morning he found 468 rocks. How many rocks did he find altogether?

   ![box] _____
   label

3. Sarah had 285 cherries. Then she bought 364 more cherries. How many total cherries does she have now?

   ![box] _____
   label

4. Noella has 563 marbles. Soniah has 255. How many more marbles does Noella have than Soniah?

   ![box] _____
   label

Mixed Addition and Subtraction Story Problems

Name _____

Homework

Directions for the puzzle appearing on page 264.

1. Start by coloring in the 7 dotted squares. These are "free" squares. They are part of the puzzle solution.

2. Solve a problem below. Then look for the answer in the puzzle grid. Color in that puzzle piece.

3. Solve all 17 problems correctly. Color in the puzzle pieces for all 17 correct answers.

4. Name the hidden picture. It is a(n) _____.

$$533 + 288$$ $$746 - 517$$ $$675 + 249$$ $$854 - 437$$

$$662 - 398$$ $$717 + 175$$ $$808 - 232$$ $$453 + 390$$

$$689 + 129$$ $$926 - 843$$ $$591 + 349$$ $$580 - 445$$

$$813 - 116$$ $$386 + 371$$ $$754 - 469$$ $$574 + 209$$ $$372 - 187$$

Homework

See page 263 for directions on how to solve the puzzle.

Spend Money

Homework

1. Use shapes to make a pattern. Draw your pattern here.

2. Use letters to describe your pattern.

_____

3. Ella bought a toy for $4.32. She paid with a $10 bill. Explain why her change will be greater than $5.

_____

_____

_____

_____

4. Yoshiro has $6. He wants to buy one toy that costs $1.98 and another toy that costs $3.75. Explain how Yoshiro can tell whether he has enough money without adding $1.98 and $3.75.

_____

_____

_____

_____

5. True or False? Similar shapes are also congruent.

Ring the answer.   True   False

Give an example to support your answer.

Name

Remembering

Add or subtract.

1.
```
  306          731         $5.64
 +499         -264        -$2.38
```

Write the hundreds, tens, and ones.

2. 471 = _____ + _____ + _____

   569 = _____ + _____ + _____

The table shows the number of days until each child's birthday. Use the table to answer exercises 3–5.

Days Until My Birthday

Name	Number of Days
Linda	200
Lupe	176
Chung	302

3. Who has to wait the longest for their birthday? _____

4. How many more days does Chung have to wait than Linda? _____

5. How many fewer days does Lupe have to wait than Linda? _____

6. **Time** On a separate piece of paper, draw what you do at 3 o'clock in the afternoon. Draw a clock face and show the time.

Use Mathematical Processes

Homework

1. Complete the table. Estimate the height of six people, pets, or objects. Find the actual heights. If necessary, round measurements to the nearest centimeter. Then, calculate the difference between your estimate and the actual measurement.

Person, Pet, or Object	Estimated Height (cm)	Actual Height (cm)	Difference Between Estimated and Actual Height (cm)

2. **On the Back** Write two questions about the data you collected. Answer your questions.

Name _____

_____

_____

_____

_____

_____

_____

_____

_____

_____

_____

_____

_____

_____

_____

_____

_____

_____

Homework

Measure four rectangular objects using your paper meter stick. Include at least two objects that have measurements greater than 100 cm. Write a clue for each object about its color, shape, location, or use. Ask your Homework Helper to guess each of your objects.

1. The length of the object is _____ cm.

The width of the object is _____ cm.

Clue: _____

_____

2. The length of the object is _____ cm.

The width of the object is _____ cm.

Clue: _____

_____

3. The length of the object is _____ cm.

The width of the object is _____ cm.

Clue: _____

_____

4. The length of the object is _____ cm.

The width of the object is _____ cm.

Clue: _____

_____

5. On the Back Use your paper meter stick to measure the height of one or more people in your family. Make a list with the name of each family member and his or her height.

Fun With Measuring

Solve the story problems. Ring *yes* or *no*.   **Show your work.**

---

1. The height of the window in Juan's
   bedroom is 2 m 3 dm. Juan found
   some curtains that are 203 cm long.
   Are the curtains long enough?

   Yes   No   Why or why not?

   _____

   _____

---

2. Max needs $2.50 to buy birthday
   cards for his twin cousins. He has
   1 dollar, 9 dimes, and 7 pennies.
   Does he have enough money?

   Yes   No   Why or why not?

   _____

   _____

---

3. Jack says that he is taller than Taci.
   Jack is 11 dm 3 cm tall. Taci is 1 m
   1 dm tall. Is Jack taller than Taci?

   Yes   No   Why or why not?

   _____

   _____

---

4. **On the Back** Measure three objects, each with a length
   greater than 100 cm. Write each length measurement
   in centimeters. Then, write the equivalent measurements
   in meters, decimeters, and centimeters.

Meter, Decimeter, and Centimeter Equivalencies

Name _____

Homework

1. Answer each question. Draw a picture if it helps.

How many dimes in 2 dollars?   How many pennies in 3 dimes?

_____   _____

How many ones in 2 tens?   How many tens in 2 hundreds?

_____   _____

How many decimeters in 2 m?   How many centimeters in 2 m?

_____   _____

How many pennies in 3 dollars?   How many ones in 4 tens?

_____   _____

2. Write the numbers.

3 m 4 dm 7 cm	___ m ___ dm ___ cm	___ m ___ dm ___ cm
= _____ dm 7 cm	= 36 dm 4 cm	= 65 dm 6 cm
= _____ cm	= _____ cm	= _____ cm
2 m 7 dm 1 cm	___ m ___ dm ___ cm	$2.48
= _____ dm 1 cm	= 43 dm 8 cm	= ___ dimes
= _____ cm	= _____ cm	___ pennies
		= _____ pennies

$6.10	$ ___ . _____
= ___ dimes ___ pennies	= ___ dimes ___ pennies
= _____ pennies	= 325 pennies

➡ **3. On the Back** Draw a line segment 10 cm long. Label
its length in decimeters. Draw another line segment
2 dm long. Label its length in centimeters.

Name _____

Homework

Is each shape two-dimensional (2-D) or
three-dimensional (3-D)?

1.

_____

2.

_____

3.

_____

For each rectangular prism, draw the top view,
front view, and side views.

4.

top	front	side

5.

top	front	side

Find the volume of each three-dimensional shape.

6.

_____ cubic units

7.

_____ cubic units

8.

_____ cubic units

⬤ **9. On the Back** Find a rectangular prism in your home.
   Trace or draw the top, front, and side views.

Name

3-Dimensional Shapes

Name _____

Homework

1. Describe how the pair of shapes is alike and different.

Shapes	How these shapes are alike	How these shapes are different

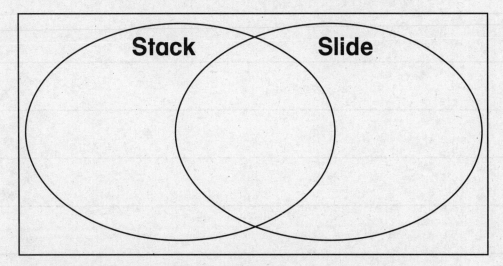

cube   sphere   cylinder   cone   rectangular prism   square pyramid

2. Use a Venn diagram to sort these shapes into two
groups: shapes that stack and shapes that slide.
Write the names of the shapes in the Venn diagram.

Stack   **Slide**

3. On the Back Find three-dimensional shapes in your
home and neighborhood. Draw the objects you find
and describe what they are used for.

Analyze 3-Dimensional Shapes **277**

ltiply.

<u> 6 </u>   <u> 8 </u>   4 × 2 = <u> 8 </u>

2 × 2 = _____

6 × 2 = _____

_____ _____ _____ _____

9 × 2 = _____

_____ _____ _____   5 × 2 = _____

ultiplication

Targeted Practice

Subtract. Ungroup if you need to.

1.
$$
\begin{array}{r}
592 \\
-475 \\
\hline
\end{array}
$$

2.
$$
\begin{array}{r}
635 \\
-464 \\
\hline
\end{array}
$$

3.
$$
\begin{array}{r}
417 \\
-246 \\
\hline
\end{array}
$$

4.
$$
\begin{array}{r}
773 \\
-527 \\
\hline
\end{array}
$$

5. $846 - 584 =$ _____

6. $934 - 417 =$ _____

Homework

Count by 3s. Then multiply.

1. Flowers on a stem

__3__ __6__ __9__ __12__   4 × 3 = __12__

2. Strawberries on a plate

___ ___ ___   3 × 3 = ____

3. Sides in triangles

___ ___ ___ ___ ___ ___   6 × 3 = ____

4. Crayons in a group

___ ___ ___ ___ ___   5 × 3 = ____

5. Toys in a sandbox play set

___ ___ ___ ___ ___ ___ ___   7 × 3 = ____

Remembering

Add or subtract.

1. $\begin{array}{r} 415 \\ +191 \\ \hline \end{array}$
2. $\begin{array}{r} 754 \\ +187 \\ \hline \end{array}$
3. $\begin{array}{r} 501 \\ -48 \\ \hline \end{array}$

Solve the story problems.   **Show your work.**

4. There are 5 trucks. Each truck has 2 logs in it.
   How many logs are there altogether?

   $2 + 2 + 2 + 2 + 2 =$ _____

   $5 \times 2 =$ _____

   ☐ _____
         label

The Mason School spring garden has 10 tulips, 8 daffodils, 11 crocuses, and 6 snowdrops. Make a table to show this. Then answer the questions. Ring *more* or *fewer*. Put a title at the top of your table.

	Number of Flowers

5. There are ☐ *more fewer* daffodils than crocuses in the Mason School garden.

6. There are ☐ *more fewer* tulips than daffodils in the Mason School garden.

7. The school needs to plant ☐ more snowdrops to have as many as there are tulips.

Groups of Three

Name _____

Homework

Count by 4s. Then multiply.

1. Wings on a dragonfly

<u>4</u>   <u>8</u>   <u>12</u>   <u>16</u>   <u>20</u> $5 \times 4 =$ <u>20</u>

2. Sides on a rectangle

___   ___   ___   ___   ___   ___ $6 \times 4 =$ ___

3. Legs on a giraffe

_____   _____   _____   _____ $4 \times 4 =$ ___

4. Fish in a frying pan

___   ___   ___   ___   ___ $5 \times 4 =$ ___

5. Apples on a plate

___   ___   ___   ___   ___   ___   ___ $8 \times 4 =$ ___

Name _____

Targeted Practice

Subtract.

1. $\begin{array}{r} 724 \\ -358 \\ \hline \end{array}$

2. $\begin{array}{r} 642 \\ -293 \\ \hline \end{array}$

3. $\begin{array}{r} 663 \\ -474 \\ \hline \end{array}$

4. $\begin{array}{r} 972 \\ -389 \\ \hline \end{array}$

5. $\begin{array}{r} 842 \\ -567 \\ \hline \end{array}$

6. $\begin{array}{r} \$5.25 \\ -\$2.38 \\ \hline \end{array}$

Name _____

Homework

Count by 5s. Then multiply.

1. Peas in a peapod

___ ___ ___ ___ $4 \times 5 =$ _____

2. Arms on a sea star

___ ___ ___ ___ ___ ___ ___ ___ ___

$9 \times 5 =$ _____

3. Leaves on a branch

___ ___ ___ ___ ___ ___ ___ $7 \times 5 =$ _____

4. Make a garden that is 5×6 or 6×5.
   Draw one bean in each square.
   How many beans are there?

   5×6 or

   $6 \times 5 =$ _____

Remembering

1. How many beans are planted in this garden?

_____ × _____ or

_____ × _____ = _____

2. Complete the money table:

68¢			
Q		=	_____ ¢
D	3	=	_____ ¢
N		=	_____ ¢
P	3	=	3¢
		=	_____ ¢

3. Write 8 equations for the Math Mountain.

_____   _____

_____   _____

_____   _____

_____   _____

Solve the story problems.

4. The boys collected 542 coats, and the girls collected 368 coats for the clothing drive. How many more coats did the boys collect than the girls?

5. Mr. Jones has 236 melons to sell at the fair. He has already sold 129. How many more melons does he have to sell?

_____
label

_____
label

Homework

1. How many apple trees are in this orchard? Write the
    4s count-bys and the total.

_____ × _____ or

_____ × _____ = _____

_____ _____ _____ _____ _____ _____ _____

2. Make an array of 32 trees. Write the multiplication.

_____ × _____ or

_____ × _____ = _____

Targeted Practice

Solve the problems. Write the count-bys and the total.

1. Leaves on a clover

___ ___ ___ ___ ___ ___ ___ ___ ___

$$9 \times 3 = \underline{\hspace{2cm}}$$

2. How many strawberries are in this carton?
Write the 4s count-bys and the total.

_____ × _____ or

_____ × _____ = _____

___ ___ ___ ___ ___ ___ ___

Name _____

Homework

Draw in your answers. Write the numbers too.

1. Valeria has **twice** as many crackers as Brian.

   Valeria has _____.

   Brian has _____.

2. Our school has **double** the number of teachers as Grant School.

   Our school has _____.

   Grant has _____.

3. Fluffy and Muffy have **equal shares** of dog treats.

   Fluffy has _____.

   Muffy has _____.

4. Main Street has **half** as many stoplights as First Street.

   Main Street has _____.

   First Street has _____.

Name _____

Remembering

Add or subtract.

1. $$\begin{array}{r} \$5.09 \\ -\$2.39 \\ \hline \end{array}$$

2. 485 + 446 = _____

Complete the number sequence.

3. 36, 41, 46 ____, ____, ____, ____, ____   Rule: n _____

Use the information in the circle graph to answer the
questions. Fill in the circle next to the correct answer.

Leaves in Joshua's Scrapbook

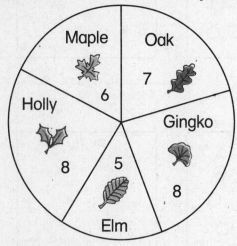

4. Joshua has the same amount of gingko
    and elm leaves as _____ and
    _____ .

    ○ maple and oak leaves
    ○ holly and maple leaves
    ○ elm and oak leaves
    ○ gingko and maple leaves

5. Joshua has 1 less maple leaf
    than _____ .

    ○ gingko leaves
    ○ holly leaves
    ○ elm leaves
    ○ oak leaves

6. Joshua has 3 more holly leaves than
    _____ .

    ○ oak leaves
    ○ elm leaves
    ○ maple leaves
    ○ gingko leaves

7. On a separate piece of paper, write a story problem
    that takes two steps to solve. Then solve it.

The Language of Shares

Name _____

Homework

Use pennies to model each problem.

1. There are 8 markers. There are 4 friends.
How can they share the markers equally?

_____ groups of _____

2. There are 18 stickers. There are 3 children.
How can they share the stickers equally?

_____ groups of _____

3. There are 24 stickers. There are 6 children.
How can they share the stickers equally?

_____ groups of _____

Solve. Use repeated subtraction.

4. How many times can you subtract
3 from 21?

The number of times you can
subtract 3 is _____.

$21 \div 3 =$ _____

$21 - 3 =$ ___
___ $- 3 =$ ___
___ $- 3 =$ ___
___ $- 3 =$ ___
___ $- 3 =$ ___
___ $- 3 =$ ___
___ $- 3 =$ ___

5. $12 \div 3 =$ _____   **6.** $25 \div 5 =$ _____   **7.** $16 \div 8 =$ _____

8. $15 \div 3 =$ _____   **9.** $24 \div 8 =$ _____   **10.** $16 \div 4 =$ _____

Name

Remembering

Add or subtract.

1. $7.09
  − $3.67

2. 378 + 254 = _____

Complete the number sequence.

3. 24, 34, ____, ____, ____, ____, ____   Rule: n _____

Use the information in the circle graph to answer the
questions. Fill in the circle next to the correct answer.

Crayon Colors in Box

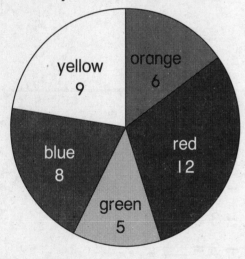

4. How many more red crayons are there
   than orange crayons?
   ◯ 18
   ◯ 7
   ◯ 6
   ◯ 5

5. There is 1 fewer blue crayon than
   _____ crayon.
   ◯ orange
   ◯ yellow
   ◯ green
   ◯ red

6. There are 7 more red crayons than
   _____ crayons.
   ◯ orange
   ◯ yellow
   ◯ blue
   ◯ green

7. On a separate piece of paper, write a story problem that takes two steps
   to solve. Then solve it.

Model Division

Homework

Name _____

Does the figure have a line of symmetry? Write
yes or *no.* If yes, draw one line of symmetry.

1.

_____

2.

_____

3.

_____

4.

_____

5.

_____

6.

_____

7.

_____

8.

_____

9.

_____

Name _____

Targeted Practice

Solve the problems.

I. How many lenses are there? Write the count-bys and the total.

___ ___ ___ ___ ___ ___ ___

$7 \times 2 =$ _____

2. How many chickens are in this barn? Write the 2s count-bys and the total.

_____ × _____ or

_____ × _____ = _____

___ ___ ___ ___ ___ ___

Symmetry

Name _____

Homework

1. Shade in the fractions for the shapes.

$$\frac{1}{2}$$

  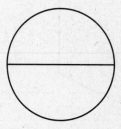

$$\frac{2}{3} = \frac{1}{3} + \frac{1}{3}$$

$$\frac{3}{4} = \frac{1}{4} + \frac{1}{4} + \frac{1}{4}$$

2. How much is shaded? Write the fraction.

 _____   _____

Name _____

Remembering

Is the figure symmetrical? Write *yes* or *no*.
If yes, draw one line of symmetry.

1.

_____

2.

_____

3.

_____

Add or subtract.

4. $7.21
   − $4.23
   _____

5. 479
   + 386
   _____

Draw in your answers. Write the numbers.

6. Sara has **double** the number
   of balloons as Ray.

   Sara has _____.

   Ray has _____.

Sara	Ray

7. Luke has **half** as many
   chips as Leda.

   Luke has _____.

   Leda has _____.

Luke	Leda

Fractions

Homework

Compare the shaded parts. Write >, <, or =.

1.

$\frac{1}{3}$ ◯ $\frac{1}{4}$

2.

$\frac{2}{4}$ ◯ $\frac{1}{2}$

3.

$\frac{1}{2}$ ◯ $\frac{3}{4}$

4.

1 ◯ $\frac{2}{3}$

Complete the chart.

	Money Amount	Number of Cents	Dollars and Cents	Fraction of a Dollar
5.	5 dimes	_____ ¢	$0.50	$\frac{5}{10}$
6.	2 dimes	20¢	$0._____	$\frac{}{10}$
7.	42 pennies	_____ ¢	$0.42	$\frac{}{100}$
8.	3 pennies	3¢	$_____._____	$\frac{}{100}$

Targeted Practice

Is the figure symmetrical? Write *yes* or *no*.
If yes, draw one line of symmetry.

1.

_____

2.

_____

3.

_____

4.

_____

5.

_____

6.

_____

7.

_____

8.

_____

Homework

Look at the bag of cubes. Circle the correct event.

1. Which event is certain?

I will pick a black cube.

I will pick a white cube.

2. Which event is impossible?

I will pick a black cube.

I will pick a white cube.

Look at the bag of cubes. How more likely or less likely are you to pick a

 than a ?

3.

more likely

less likely

4.

more likely

less likely

Color in the spinners to make the statements true.

5. This is a fair spinner.

6. This is an unfair spinner.

Name _____

Remembering

Use the information in the bar graph to
answer the questions.

School Supplies Sold on Monday

1. How many pencils and erasers
were sold altogether?

_____

2. How many fewer notebooks were
sold than erasers?

_____

3. How many more boxes of crayons were sold
than calculators?

_____

4. How many fewer pencils need to be sold to
equal the number of notebooks sold?

_____

Subtract.

5.   584
      − 275

6.   427
      − 136

7.   912
      − 458

8.   203
      − 171

9. Time On a separate piece of paper, draw what you do
at 12 o'clock P.M. Show the time on a digital clock.

Explore Probability

Homework

Make an organized list to solve each problem.

Show your work.

1. Eli has a blue shirt and a tan shirt. He also has a pair of black pants and a pair of brown pants. How many different combinations of a shirt and pants can he wear?

   ☐ different combinations

Shirt Color		Pants Color
blue	⟶	black
blue	⟶	
tan	⟶	

2. Mr. Alvarez has lilies, roses, and tulips to put in a tall vase and in a short vase. How many different combinations can he arrange with the flowers and vases?

   ☐ different combinations

Flower		Vase
lilies	⟶	tall
lilies	⟶	
roses	⟶	

3. Blair packed a pair of boots and a pair of running shoes. She also packed a baseball cap, a sun hat, and a western hat. How many different combinations of shoes and hats can she wear?

   ☐ different combinations

Shoe	Hat

Targeted Practice

1. Shade in the fractions for the shapes.

$$\frac{2}{3} = \frac{1}{3} + \frac{1}{3}$$

$$\frac{3}{4} = \frac{1}{4} + \frac{1}{4} + \frac{1}{4}$$

2. How much is shaded? Write the fraction.

 _____   _____

Possible Outcomes
Homework

1. Suppose you win a prize if the spinner lands on the cat.

1   2   3

Which spinner should you choose? Why?

_____

_____

2. Draw a spinner with 2 colors where you would be twice as likely to get red than green.

3. Draw a spinner with 3 colors where you would be twice as likely to get red than green.

4. Carol has $10. Soo Min has half the amount of money that Carol has. Pedro has 4 times the amount of money that Soo Min has. How much money does Pedro have? Explain.

_____

_____

_____

5. Alberto has 4 oranges. David has 3 times as many oranges as Alberto. Hana has half the number of oranges that David has. How many oranges does Hana have?

_____

_____

_____

Name _____   **Date** _____

Remembering

Is the figure symmetrical? Write *yes* or *no*.
If yes, draw one line of symmetry.

1.   2.   3.

_____   _____   _____

Subtract.

4.
$$854 - 149$$ $$635 - 282$$ $$736 - 479$$ $$905 - 534$$

Draw in your answers. Write the numbers.

5. Pablo has **double** the number
   of counters as Mio.

   Pablo has _____.

   Mio has _____.

Pablo	Mio

6. Jason has **half** as many
   counters as Lupe.

   Jason has _____.

   Lupe has _____.

Jason	Lupe

Use Mathematical Processes

Name _____

Homework

1. Use the width of your hand to measure the length of three objects. Measure the same objects using the width of a finger.

Object	Length (hands)	Length (fingers)

2. Find three containers. Use small objects, like beans or cups of rice or water, to measure the capacity of each container. Remember to include units in your answers.

Container	Capacity

3. Find three objects that are about the same size. Hold the objects one at a time to compare their masses. List the objects in order from least to greatest mass.

_____

_____

_____

4. **On the Back** Describe how measuring length and capacity are similar.

_____

_____

_____

_____

_____

_____

_____

_____

_____

_____

_____

_____

_____

_____

_____

Explore Measurement Concepts

Name _____

Homework

1. Find five objects at home to measure in inches.
   Estimate and measure the length of each object.
   If necessary, round the measurements. Complete
   the table.

Object	Estimated length (in.)	Measured length (in.)

2. Find five objects at home to measure in feet or yards.
   Complete the table. Remember to include units with
   your measurements.

Object	Measured length

3. Fill in the correct number.

   1 ft = _____ in.   3 ft = _____ yd   1 yd = _____ in.

   2 yd = _____ ft   3 ft = _____ in.   36 in. = _____ ft

4. **On the Back** Measure your height in feet. Measure
   the length of your leg and the length of your arm in
   inches. Make a drawing of yourself. Write the
   measurements on your drawing.

Name

Homework

Ring the correct tool for each problem.

1. Paul wants to know the width of a box.

2. Ria wants to know the weight of an apple.

3. Dabbt wants to follow a recipe that needs 1 cup of milk.

4. Put the containers in order from the one that holds the greatest to the one that holds the least.

_____   _____   _____   _____

5. How many cups equal a pint? _____

6. How many pints equal a quart? _____

7. How many quarts equal a gallon? _____

8. On the Back   Draw 3 objects that should be weighed in ounces and 3 that should be weighed in pounds.

Measurement

Name _____

Homework

Write the value of each. Then ring the set with the greater value.

1.

_____   _____

2.

_____   _____

3.

_____   _____

Order the coin sets from **least** to **greatest.**

4.

_____   _____   _____

5. On the Back Draw 3 groups of coins. Order the sets of coins from greatest to least.

Homework

Homework

Use the 120 Poster on the back.
Skip count forward and backward.

1. Start at 0. Skip count forward by 5s.
Color each box yellow.

2. Start at 100. Skip count backward by 5s.
Put a blue dot in each box.

3. Start at 0. Skip count forward by 10s.
Circle each box.

4. Start at 100. Skip count backward by 10s.
X each box.

5. Start at 15. Skip count forward by 5s.

15, _____, _____, _____, _____, _____, _____, _____, _____, _____

6. Start at 95. Skip count backward by 5s.

95, _____, _____, _____, _____, _____, _____, _____, _____, _____

7. Start at 8. Skip count forward by 10s.

8, _____, _____, _____, _____, _____, _____, _____, _____, _____

8. Start at 92. Skip count backward by 10s.

92, _____, _____, _____, _____, _____, _____, _____, _____, _____

Name _____

1	2	3	4	5	6	7	8	9	10
11	12	13	14	15	16	17	18	19	20
21	22	23	24	25	26	27	28	29	30
31	32	33	34	35	36	37	38	39	40
41	42	43	44	45	46	47	48	49	50
51	52	53	54	55	56	57	58	59	60
61	62	63	64	65	66	67	68	69	70
71	72	73	74	75	76	77	78	79	80
81	82	83	84	85	86	87	88	89	90
91	92	93	94	95	96	97	98	99	100
101	102	103	104	105	106	107	108	109	110
111	112	113	114	115	116	117	118	119	120

120 Poster (front)

Homework

Use the line graph to answer the questions.

Average Monthly Sales

1. What is the title of the graph? _____

2. How much time does this graph represent? _____

3. What change is happening over the months? _____

4. How much did the sales increase between January and February? _____

5. How much did the sales increase between February and March? _____

6. Between which two months did the sales stay the same? _____

7. Between which two months did the sales rise the most? _____

8. **On the Back** Write and answer your own question about the graph.

Name _____

_____

_____

_____

_____

_____

_____

_____

_____

_____

_____

_____

_____

_____

_____

Name _____

Homework

Use three-dimensional shapes or think about which ones you would use.

1. Name 2 ways to make a tree.
List the shapes you used and how many.

_____

_____

2. Name 2 ways to make a house.
List the shapes you used and how many.

_____

_____

Name the shape(s) you can cut to make the named shapes.

3. 2 rectangular prisms

_____

4. 3 cylinders

_____

5. 4 cubes

_____

6. On the Back Draw 3 different three-dimensional shapes.
Draw a shape you can make by combining the 3 shapes.

Homework

Name _____

Explore 3-Dimensional Shapes

@ Flavie
Stamantopolos

Alanie
Stamanfopollos